Big Sailor

My First Big ABC

Ages 3-5

Vol.2 D·E·F

Onionidu!
Your study buddy

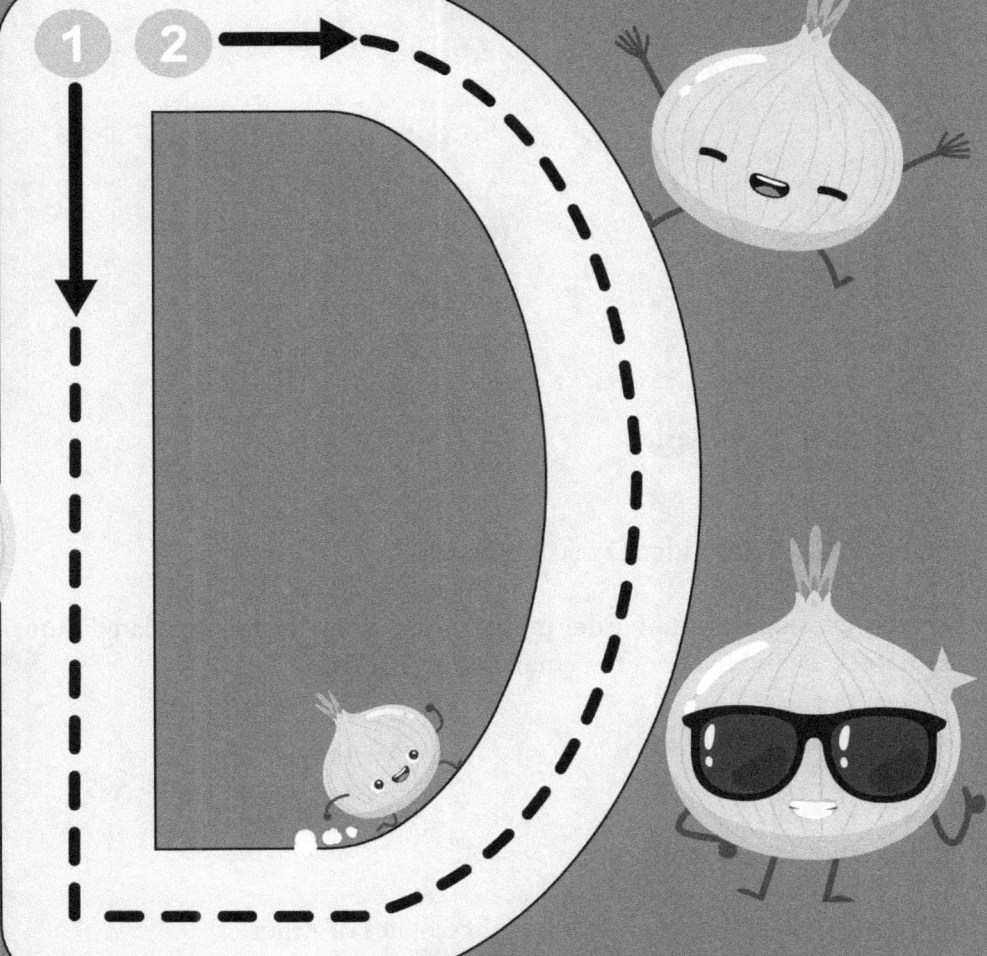

My First Big ABC Book Series
Big Sailor Edu

Copyright © 2021 Cambridge Dynasty Press

For permission requests, bulk order information, or any busine ss related inquries, please contact the publisher at the email address below.

Cambridge Dynasty Press
30 N Gould St. STE4000
Sheridan, WY 82801
Email: Bestsailoredu@Gmail.com

Written, Designed, and Printed in the United States of America

978-1-7357844-4-1(Paperback)

47678459

Hi! Nice to meet you.
My name is Onionidu!

I am your study buddy for this book!

1. Building Skills for Pen Control
2. Recognizing Alphabet Letters
3. Building Confidence
4. Enjoying a Good Book
5. Being Patient with Practice
6. Developing Creative Thinking
7. Being Proud of Achievement
8. Having Fun

This book belongs to

_____
(name)

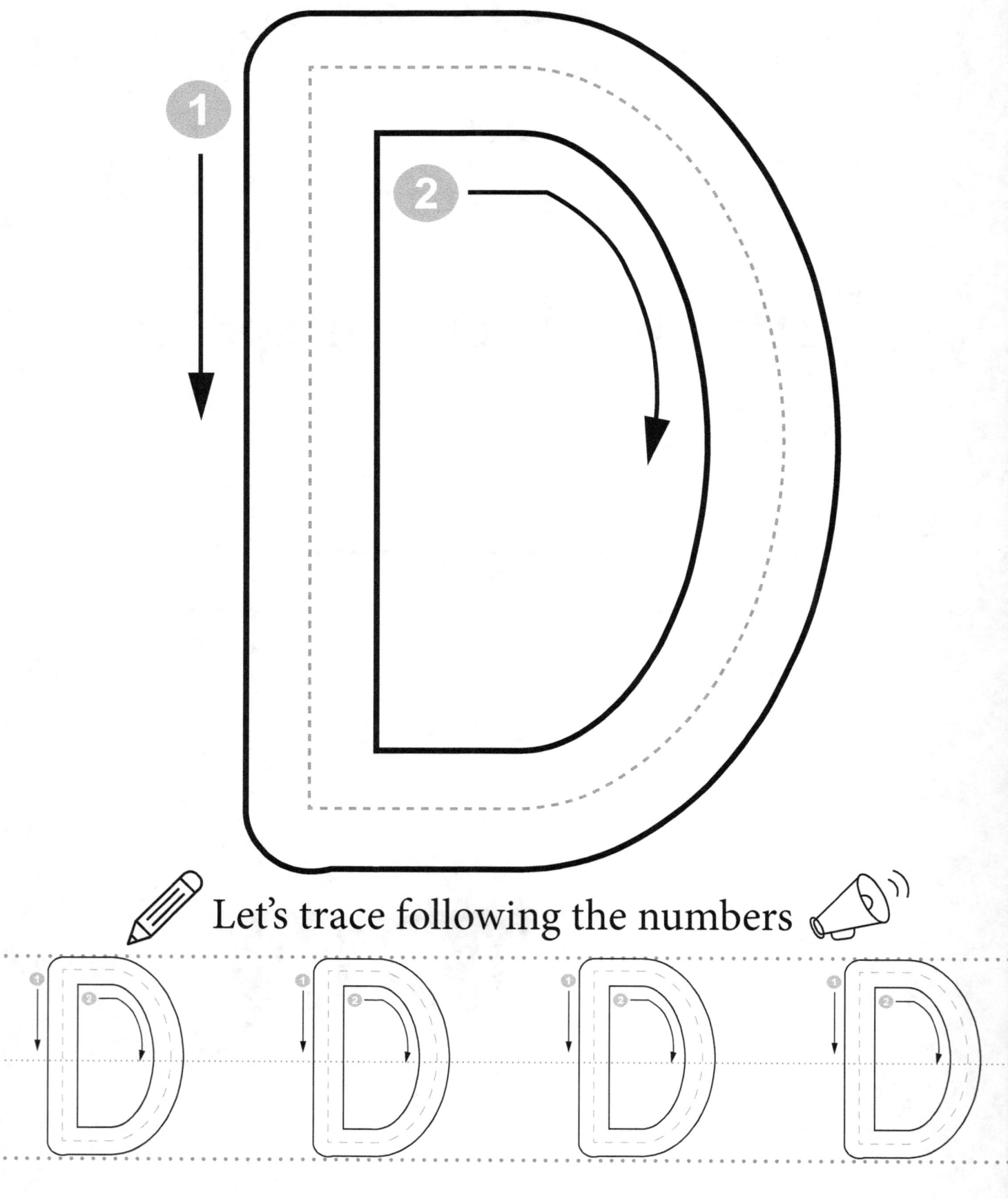

Let's trace following the numbers

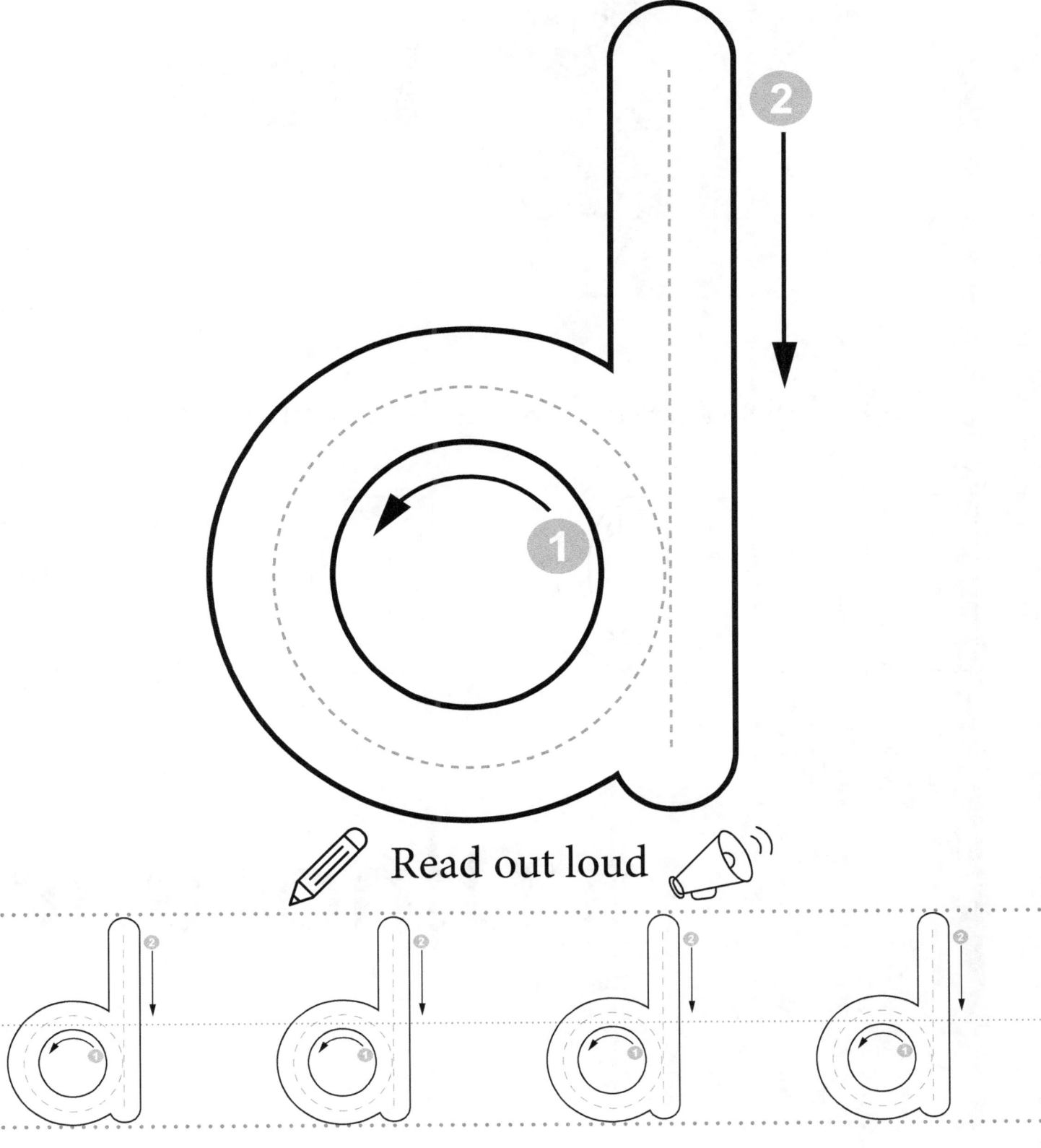

Read out loud

# Dog

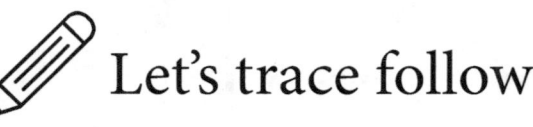 Let's trace following the numbers

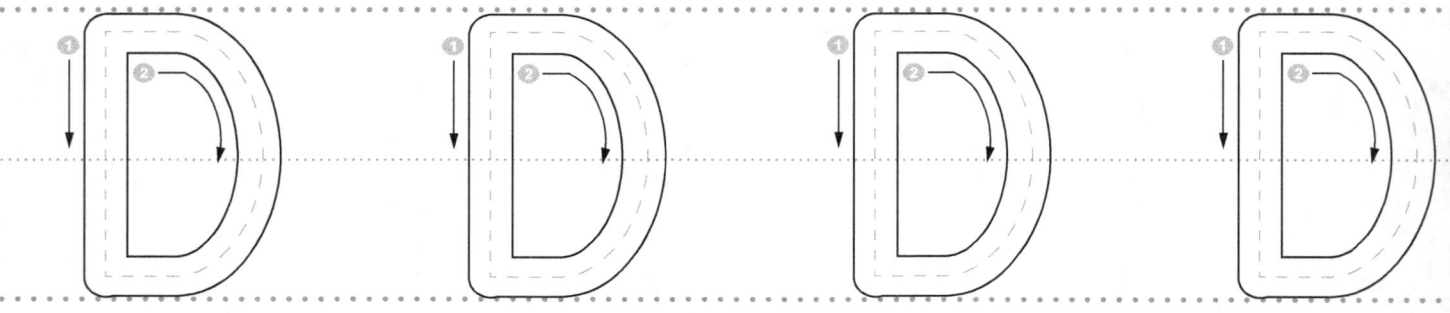

# Dinosaur

drum

✏️ Read out loud 📢

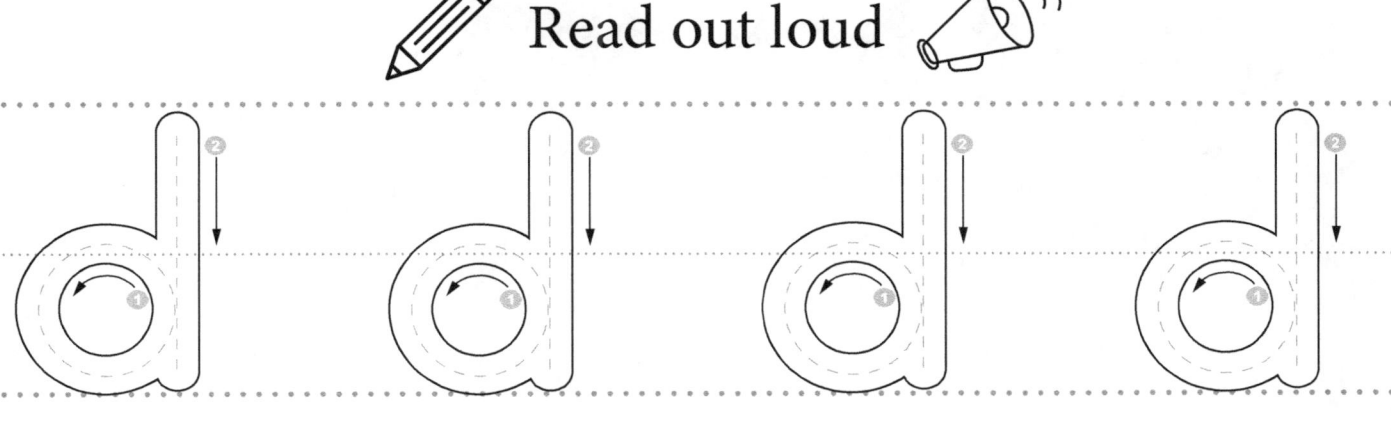

duck

Find every D and color them

Trace the dotted line and read out loud

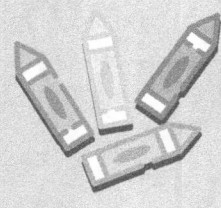 # Find every D and color the sections

Onionidu

Find every d and circle them

d for dog

Trace the dotted line and read out loud

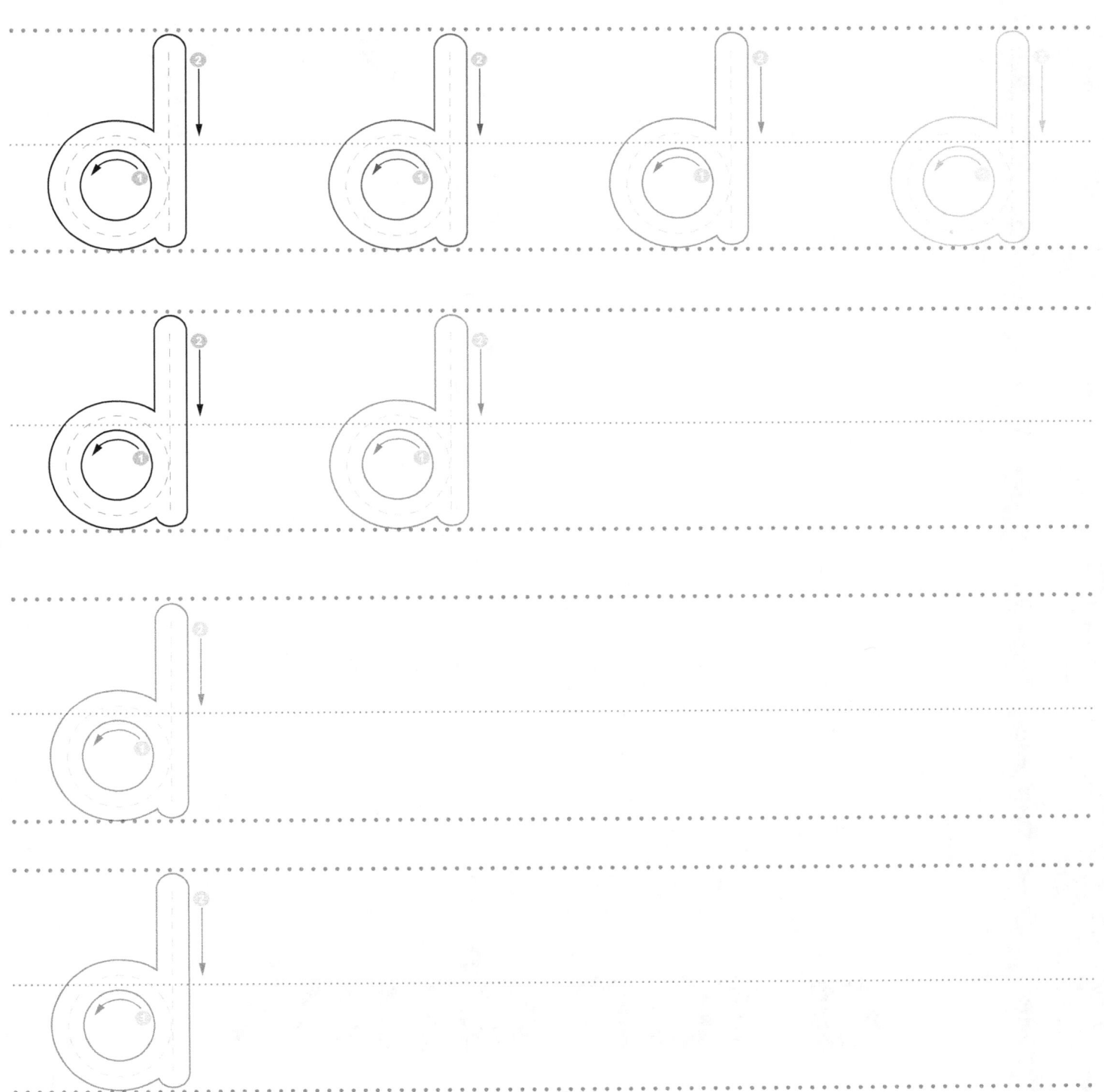

d for duck

Draw lines to match

 **Find every d and color the sections**

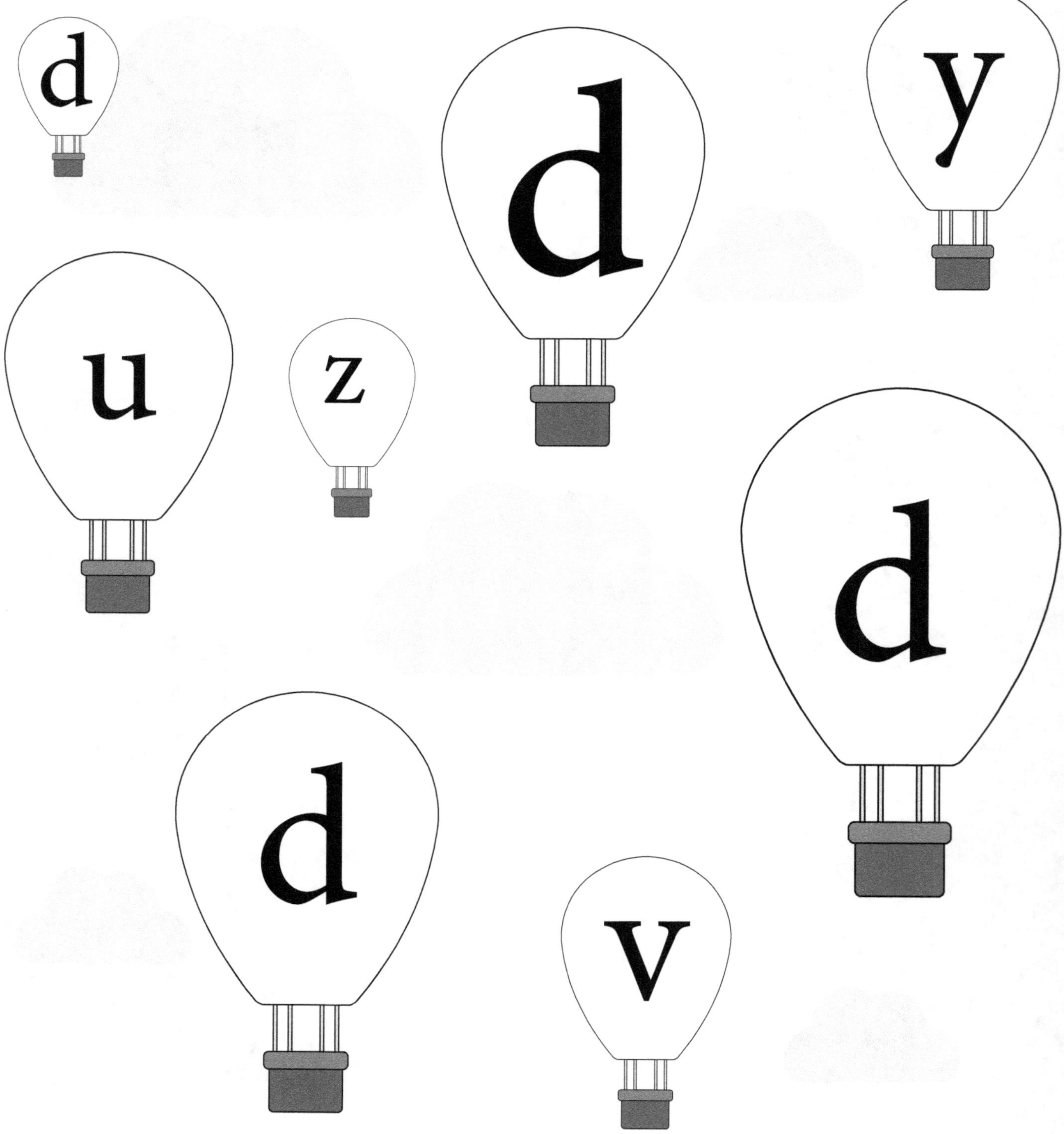

Trace the dotted line and read out loud

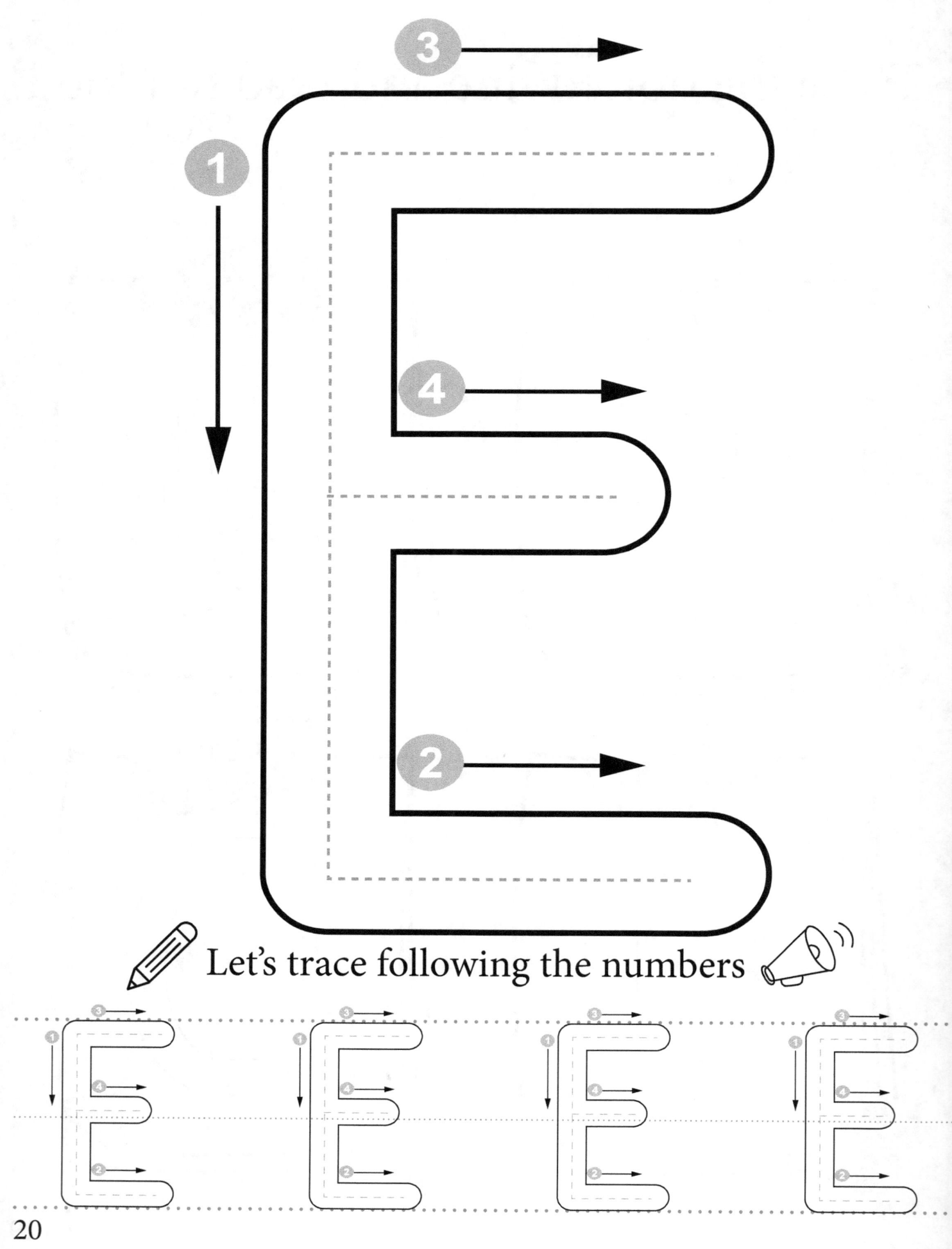

Let's trace following the numbers

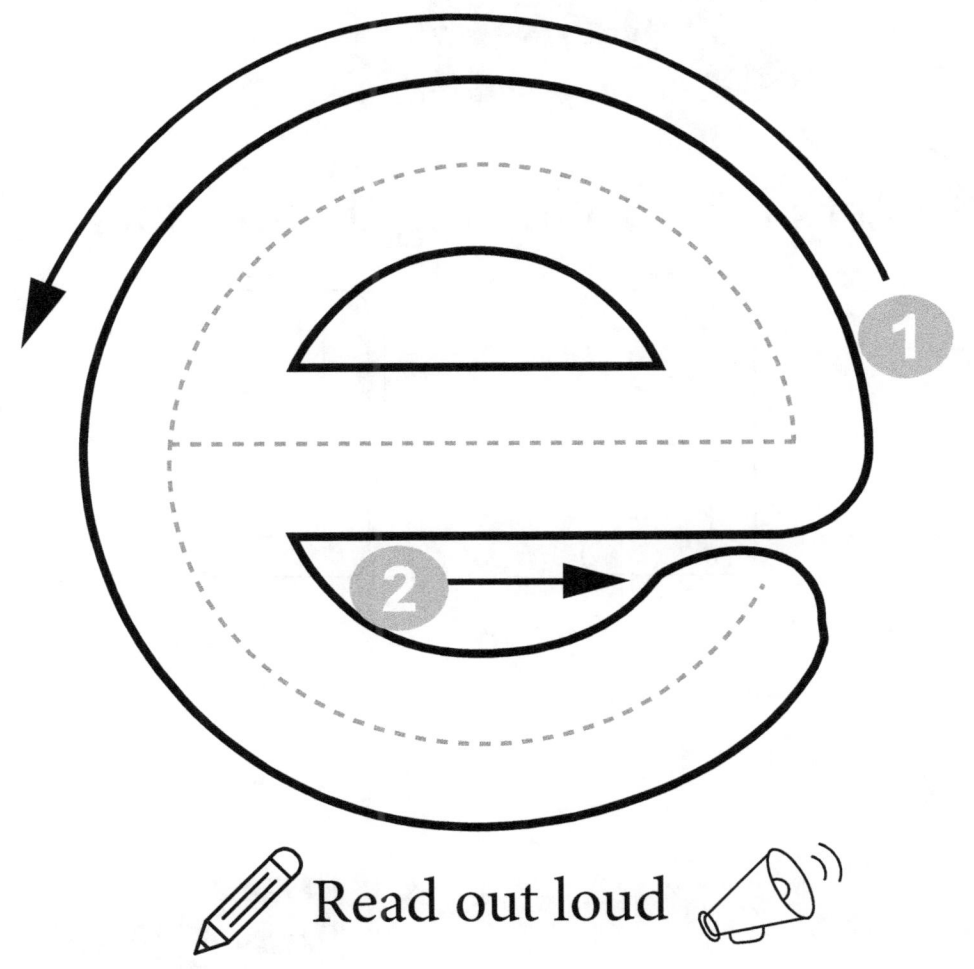

✏️ Read out loud 📣

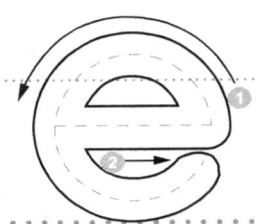 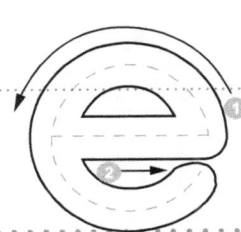 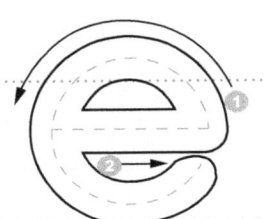 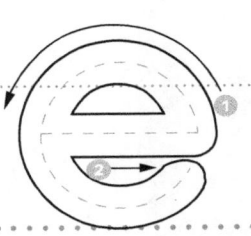

Elephant

✏️ Let's trace following the numbers 📣

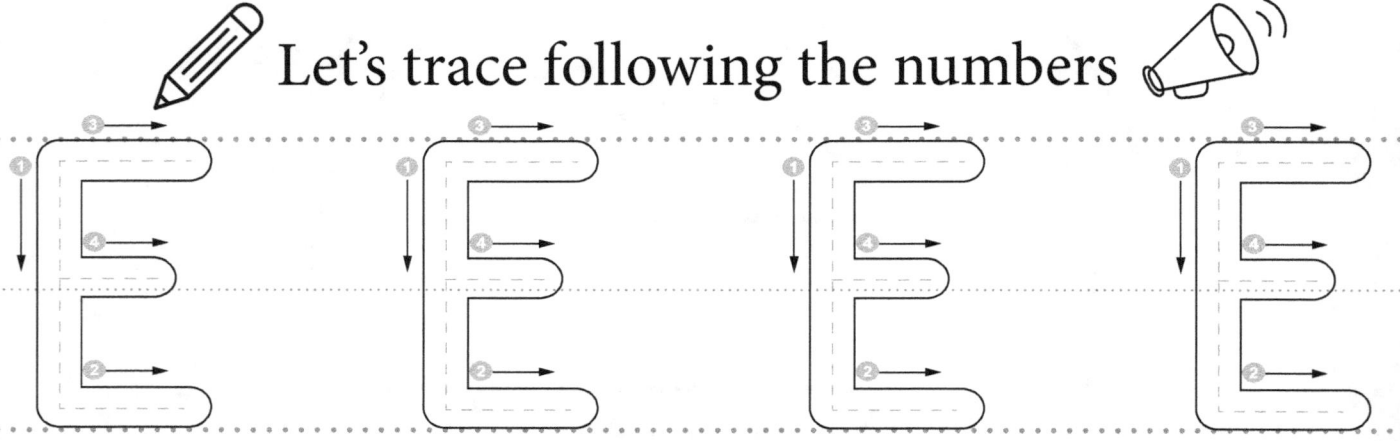

Ear

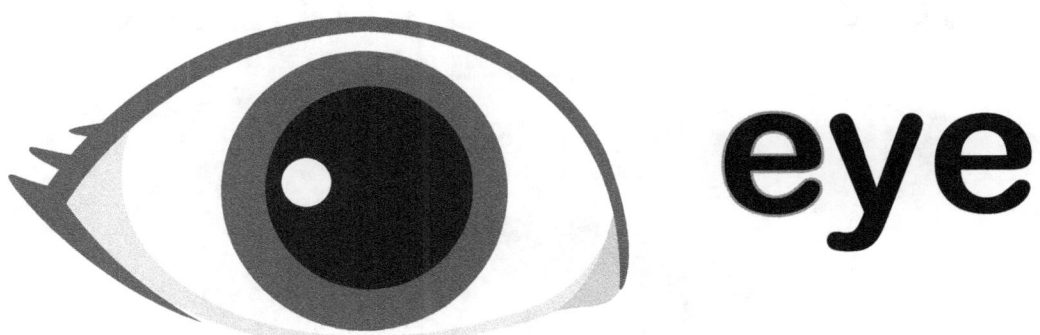

eye

 Read out loud

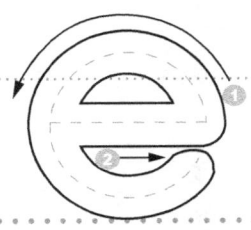 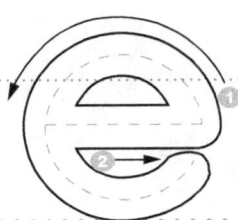 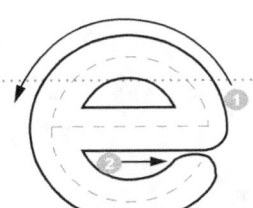 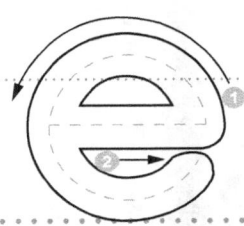

egg

Find every E and color them

FEELING MOTIVATED.

You are doing amazing!

Trace the dotted line and read out loud

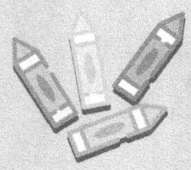

Find every E and color the sections

Onionidu

Find every e and circle them

e for egg

Trace the dotted line and read out loud

Draw lines to match

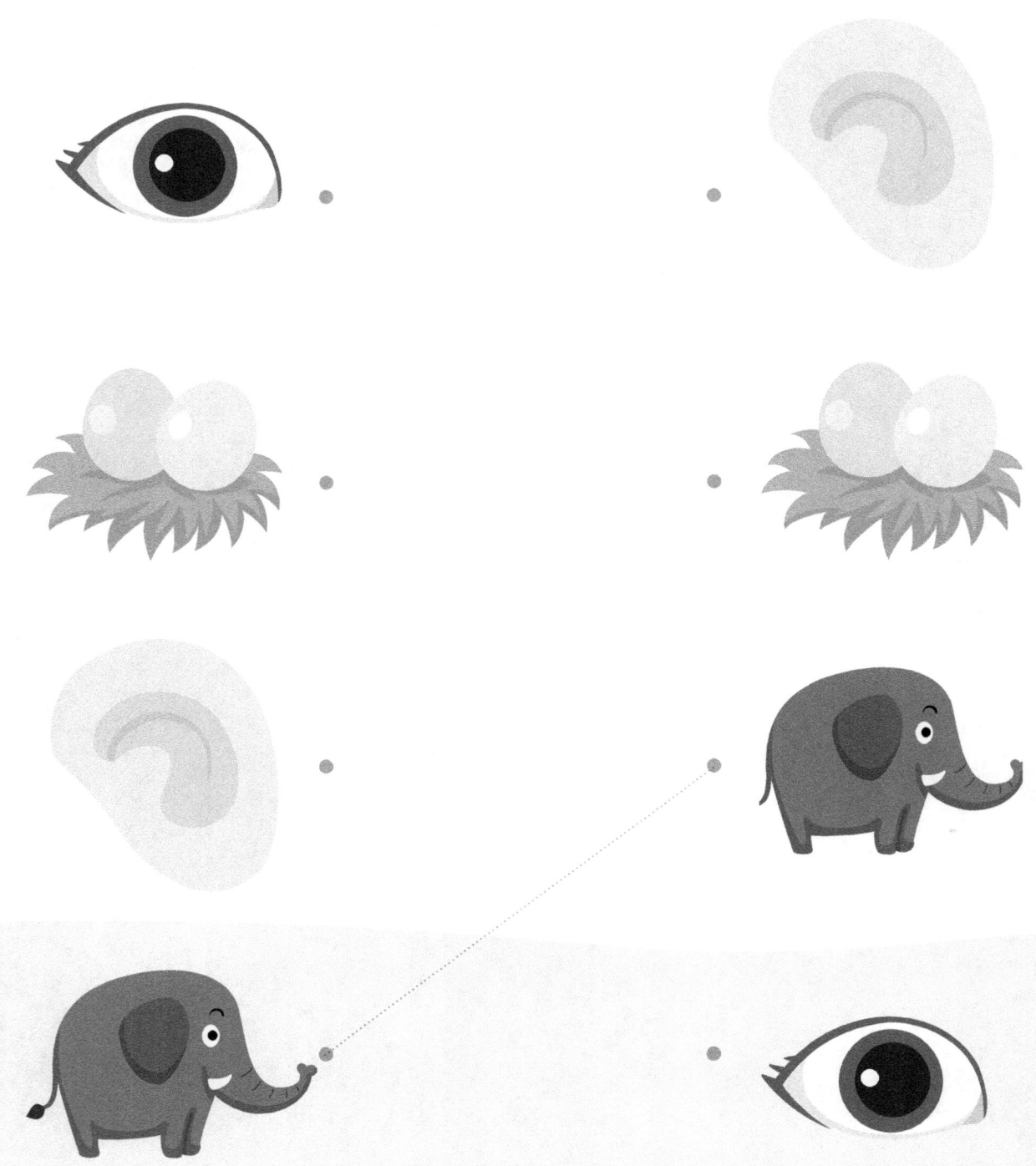

e for elephant

 **Find every e and color the sections**

Trace the dotted line and read out loud

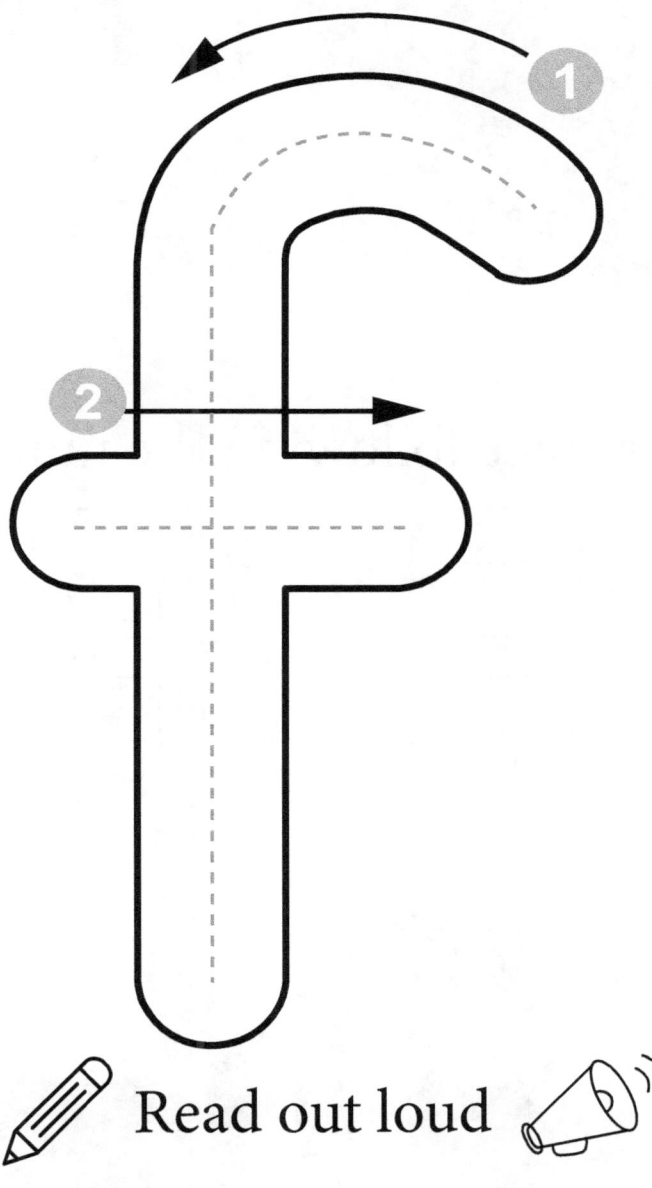

Read out loud

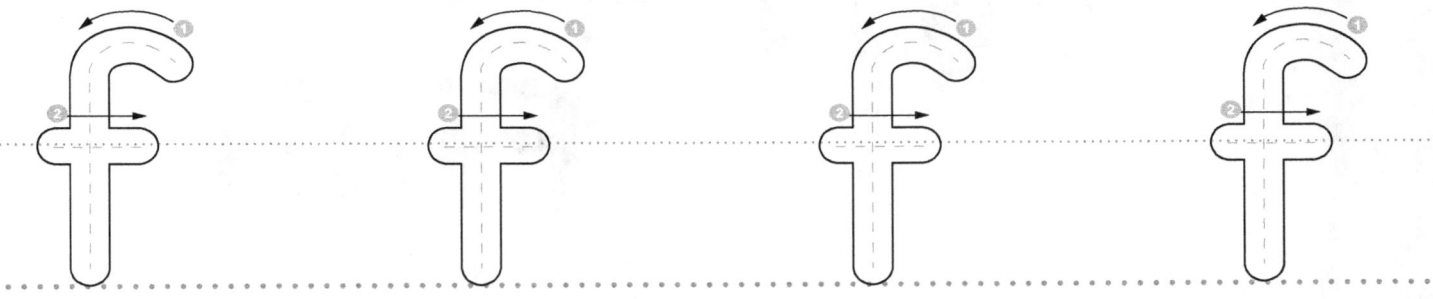

fork

 Read out loud

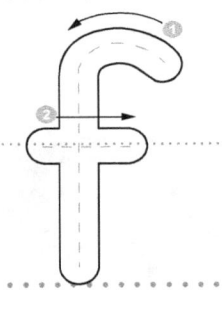 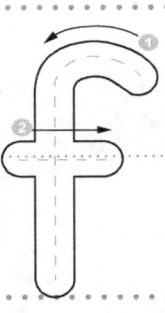 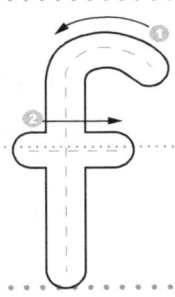 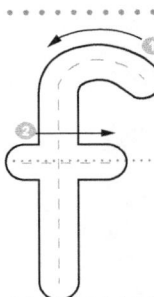

fox

Find every F and color them

Trace the dotted line and read out loud

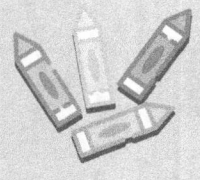

Find every F and color the sections

Onionidu

Trace the dotted line and read out loud

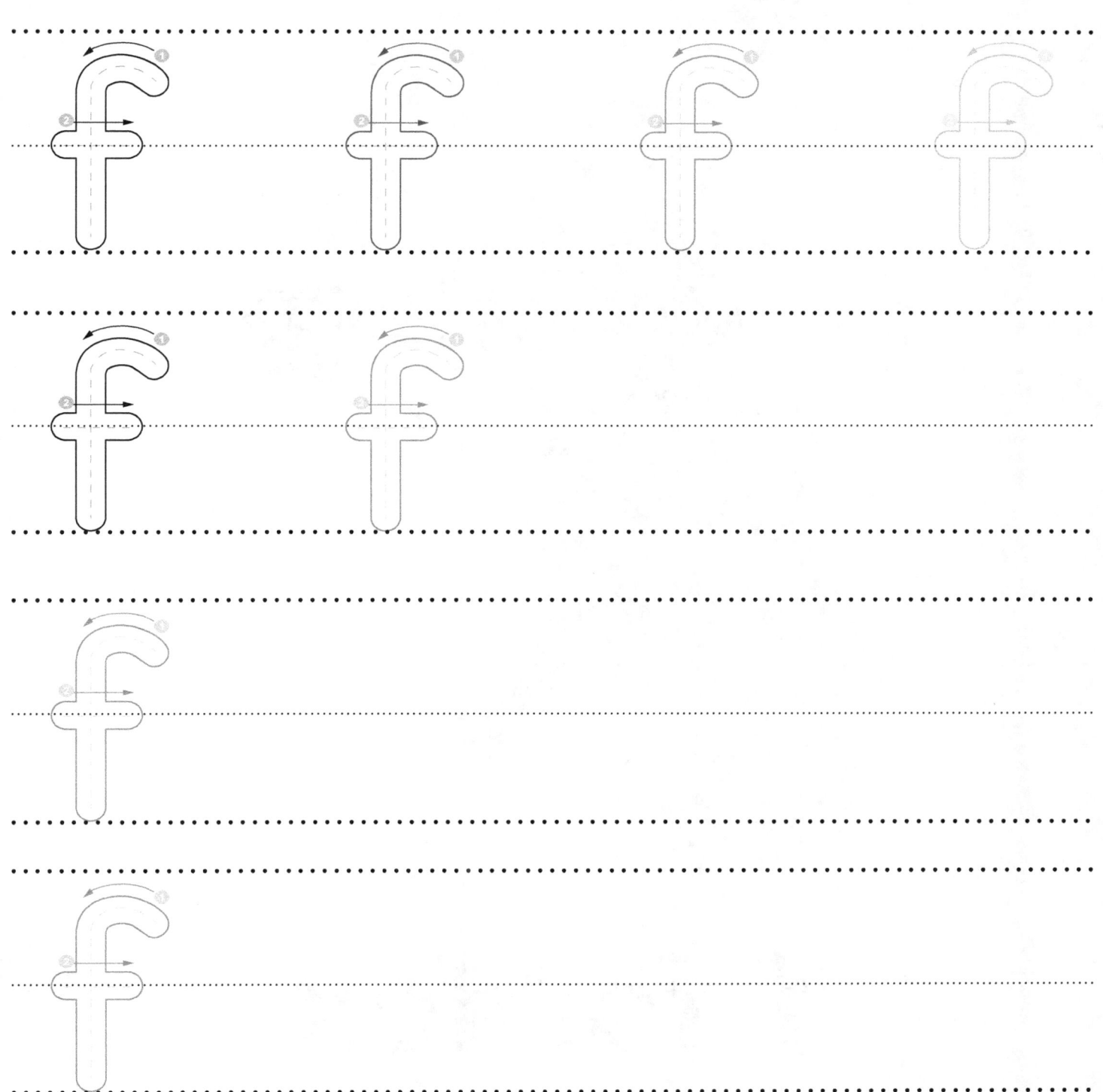

f for fox

Draw lines to match

 **Find every f and color the sections**

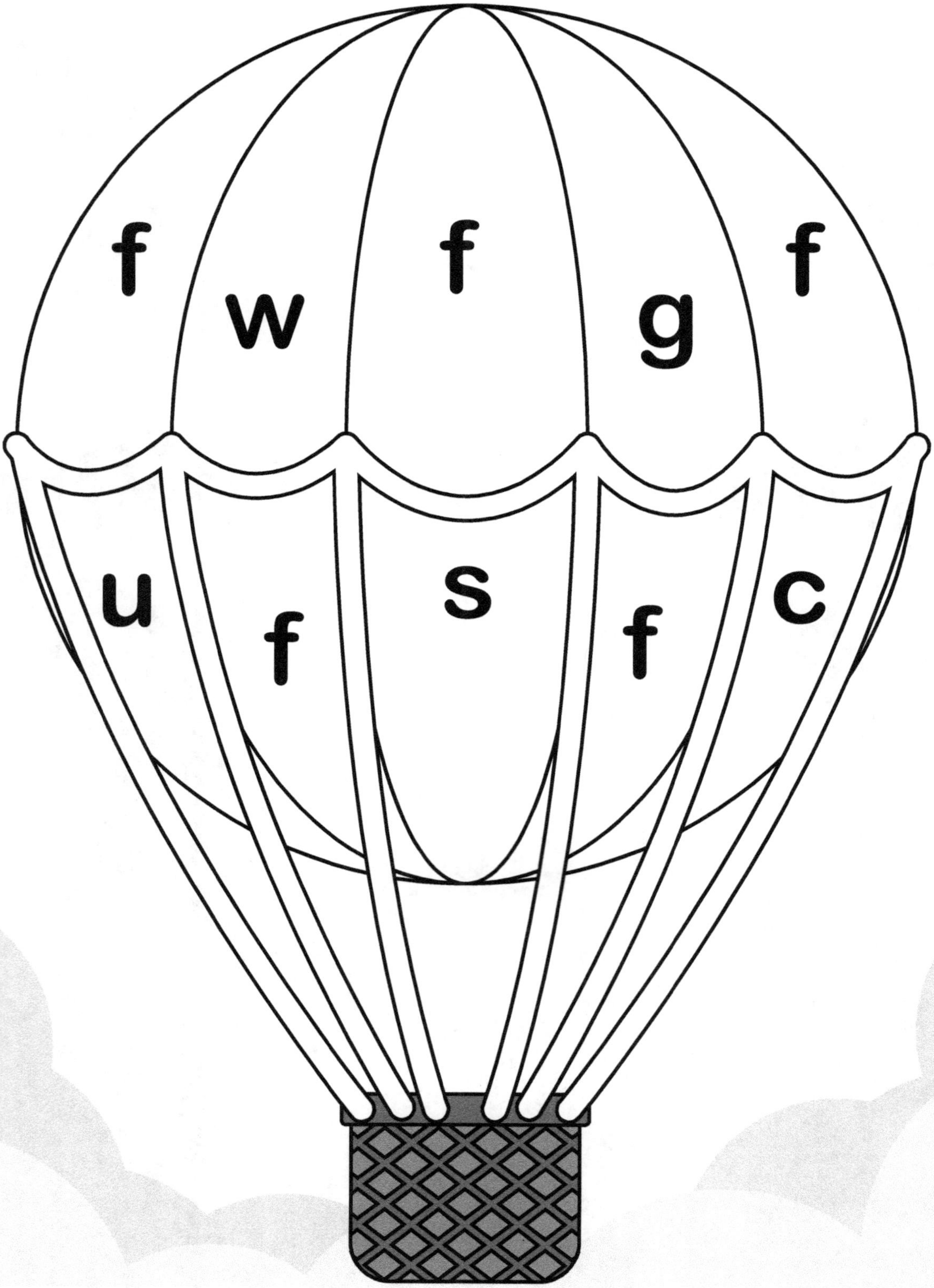

Trace the dotted line and read out loud

Where is Onionidu?

Find and circle!

Let's express your

I am cool

I am hungry

I am playful

I am proud

I am okay

feelings with Onionidu!

Let's express your

I am sad

I am calm

I am rushing

I am frustrated

I am angry

feelings with Onionidu!

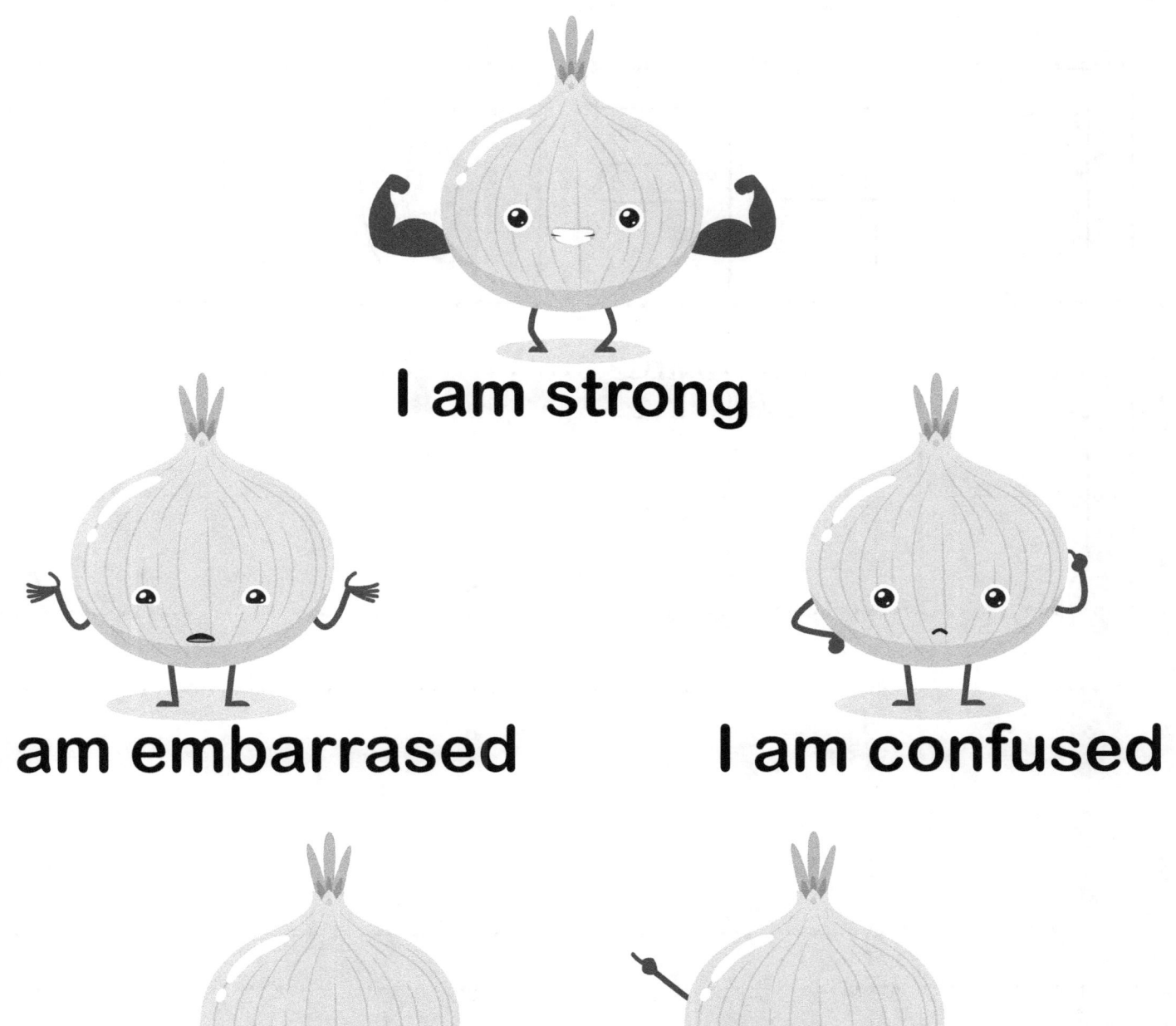

I am strong

I am embarrased

I am confused

I am shy

I am brave

Write DEF and read out loud

DEF DEF

DEF

DEF

DEF

Write def and read out loud

d e f d e f

d e f

d e f

d e f

Award
You are amazing!

This award is for

_____ _____
(first name)   (last name)

Great job finishing the book!

Date: _____

Visit Our Website

BigSailorEdu.com

and Get Free & Fun

Educational Material

ABC Workbook Series by Big Sailor Edu

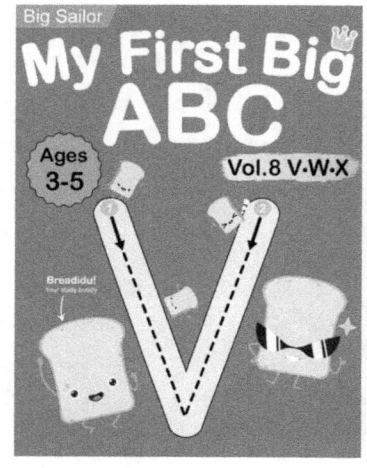

Cambridge Dynasty Press

www.ingramcontent.com/pod-product-compliance
Lightning Source LLC
Chambersburg PA
CBHW081421080526
44589CB00016B/2627